*TALKING* **STONE**

# TALKING STONE

## ROCK ART OF THE COSOS

Paul Goldsmith

THE UNIVERSITY OF UTAH PRESS

*Salt Lake City*

The Defiance House Man colophon is a registered trademark of The University of Utah Press. It is based on a four-foot-tall Ancient Puebloan pictograph (late PIII) near Glen Canyon, Utah.

21 20 19 18 17     1 2 3 4 5

Library of Congress Cataloging-in-Publication Data
Names: Goldsmith, Paul (Cinematographer), author, photographer.
Title: Talking stone : rock art of the Cosos / Paul Goldsmith.
Description: Salt Lake City : The University of Utah Press, [2017] | Includes
  bibliographical references.
Identifiers: LCCN 2016040700 | ISBN 9781607815518 (pbk. : alk. paper)
  ISBN 9781607815525 (e-book)
Subjects: LCSH: Panamint Indians--California—Coso Range—Antiquities. |
  Petroglyphs—California—Coso Range. | Coso Range (Calif—Antiquities. |
  Rock paintings—California—Coso Range. | Indian art—California—Coso
  Range.
Classification: LCC E78.C15 G57 2017 | DDC 979.4/87—dc23
LC record available at https://lccn.loc.gov/2016040700

All photographs are copyright Paul Goldsmith, except as noted below.
"Owens Valley Paiute Dwellings," INF 499, page 20, lower. Courtesy of County of
  Inyo, Eastern California Museum.
"Mica Effigy of High Desert Ram," page 33, artifact courtesy of Gilmer L. Brush.
"Bighorn Sheep Shrine at Rose Spring Site," drawing Michael W. Chittock, page 70.
Don Austin photographs of petroglyphs, page 11, right; page 16; page 25, lower;
  page 57; page 67; page 92, upper. Courtesy of Evelyn Austin.

Printed and bound in Korea.

# CONTENTS

# INTRODUCTION

**HIDDEN IN THE CANYONS** of a vast and highly restricted military base on the edge of the Mojave Desert is the largest concentration of rock art in North America—possibly in the world.

For thousands of years, a now-vanished culture created images of animals, shamans, and abstract forms. The most prevalent motif by far is the bighorn sheep: over 20,000 are pecked into the rocks.

It is generally agreed that the last culture to make the petroglyphs (images pecked in stone) had mysteriously disappeared or moved on. Some of the rock art may date back ten thousand years, but approximately 800 years ago it stopped.

What happened to the creators of these images? Maybe they dwindled because of drought, or an incoming group killed or absorbed them, or perhaps they migrated to another part of the Southwest. We don't even know their name. Today we call them the Coso because the Native Americans who live in the area now (the Kawaiisu and Western Shoshone) gave the long-gone people that name. There is a thermal site with steam and hot springs near the rock-art canyons. "Coso" is their word for steam, so Coso became the name for the long-gone ancient people.

The Coso probably never numbered more than about 500. Why did so few create some many images? What was their purpose? Why was the making of petroglyphs apparently so important to them?

All that is clear is the Coso are gone, but their images, carefully pecked in stone, remain.

Renegade Canyon, one of the half dozen canyons that contain the most petroglyphs, looking west to the eastern Sierra.

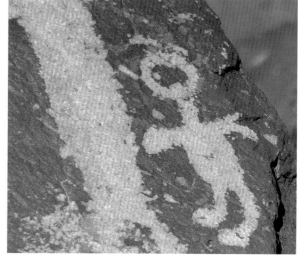

What was once the home of the Coso is now almost entirely on land the U.S. Navy acquired before World War II for weapons testing. Since target practice is difficult on the water, the Navy needed a vast, empty wilderness. The 1.1 million acres of desert, canyons, dry lakes, and mountains that are known as China Lake were perfect. When the Navy discovered that its new test site was also home to an extraordinary collection of rock art, it was easily able to avoid damaging those canyons. Today the Navy is proud protector and curator of the Coso images. Getting onto the base without permission is flatly impossible, so these areas are now some of the most untouched and protected in North America.

In 2012, I approached the Navy to film a documentary on the rock art, and along with archaeologist Alan Gold I was eventually granted access to the petroglyph canyons. Although the ongoing weapons testing did not affect these areas, we had to cross most of the base to reach them. There were very few days when that could be arranged safely. Weather was also a factor: snow in the winter and extreme heat in the summer. And even though we were in the desert, our trips were cancelled more than once because of flash floods. Yet the more I learned about China Lake and the rock art there, the more I came to see how unique these sites are. Since we had gained access, I thought a book would be appropriate as well as a film.

Both the film and the book share the Coso images and explore a little of their origin and possible meaning. In this regard, I thought it would be appropriate to hear multiple voices. I reached out to Native Americans, as well as anthropologists, hunters, an artist, and a psychologist. But in the end, I aim to keep interpretations of the petroglyphs to a minimum so as not to diminish their mystery, magic, and power. I hope readers will be able to encounter these images with fresh eyes and form their own opinions.

# THE BEGINNING OF THE SEARCH

**ONCE THE NAVY GRANTED** us permission, we were led into the canyons by base archaeologist Mike Baskerville. He was quick to point out that this small area was home to ten thousand years of weapons technology, starting from the simplest spear and continuing up through the most futuristic missiles and drones. He thought it an amazing coincidence that it all took place in this particular rugged geography.

Yesterday's weapons were one thing, but we weren't going to be permitted to see any of the modern stuff. Once through the base gates and security, we had to stow our cameras, even though we could only see what looked like igloos and occasional, blasted objects of indeterminate nature. After an hour's drive up out of the dry lakebed and into the mountain canyons, we began to hike.

Alan Gold, anthropologist and author.

Mike Baskerville, cultural resource manager, Naval Air Weapons Station China Lake.

Once we dropped down into the canyons, we saw rock art everywhere. The canyon walls were, at most, one or two hundred feet high, with a jumble of boulders and rockfall rising from the base. The basalt stone was almost black with desert varnish: the accumulation of iron and manganese deposited over thousands of years. The Coso made their petroglyphs by pecking this varnish off to reveal the brighter, lighter-colored rock underneath. Unlike pictographs, which are painted on rocks, petroglyphs last for thousands of years until the desert varnish gradually reclaims them. Even then they can be faintly discerned when viewed from just the right angle.

Left: These images are fully repatinated and can only be seen from this angle. Little Lake is in the background.

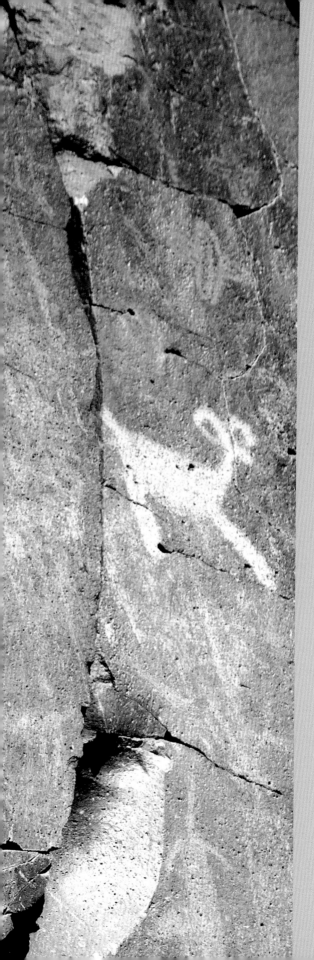

# WHO MADE THESE IMAGES?

**ALAN GOLD THINKS THAT** the Coso were never very numerous. He believes that, even in prehistoric times with highest precipitation, the China Lake environment wouldn't have supported more than 500 people. Yet this only deepens the mystery, and Alan has spent his career pursuing the question why such a small group created so many images.

The Coso would have lived in small bands as hunter-gatherers, moving from the lowlands in the winter gradually into the pines near the mountaintops where they gathered pinyon nuts. Along the way they inhabited temporary campsites, hunting and gathering plants, roots, and seeds. Their house rings are still clearly visible today, along with the metates they used for grinding seeds, undisturbed for hundreds of years. The campsites are on the flats above the canyons and are not closely or obviously connected. Aside from the manos and metates, some broken points, and many obsidian flakes, there's not much beyond the rock art to help reconstruct their world. No graves, no pottery, no baskets. Besides the rock art, they left few traces.

The remains of a hut ring and broken metates. The ring of stones would have been the foundation for a structure of wood. When occupied, the site would have looked much like the historic-period Shoshone campsite seen in the figure above.

Alan and I came across one of the quartz stones that the Coso used as a tool to peck away the varnish to make rock art.

The Kawaiisu, one of the tribes that have lived in the same general area in historic times, have a scary figure called "Grasshopper Man." Could this be an ancient ancestor?

California quail. This quail has an unusual, teardrop-shaped, forward-drooping head plume. The plume, or topknot, is more pronounced in males.

The same distinctive quail plume is seen in the headdress of the figure in foreground.

An atlatl in action. This ancient spear-throwing device extended the reach of the throwing arm, giving greater leverage and power.

# THE ATLATL

**BEFORE THE BOW AND** arrow, there was the atlatl, a spear-throwing device. The atlatl existed long before humans came to the New World and presumably came with the first inhabitants at least 15,000 years ago. In the Coso rock art, we can see stylized images of atlatls all along the canyon rocks. The atlatl gave a hunter greater leverage when he threw his spear, providing more power and distance. The whole atlatl-spear combination was a delicate piece of technology and certainly an improvement on basic thrusting or hurling.

The atlatl had a tiny hook on the launching end to engage the spear, a finger grip on the handle for the hunter to grasp, and a small, flat rock mounted near the middle, presumed to be a balancing weight. Whatever the purpose, the weights are often portrayed in the rock art much larger and far out of proportion when compared to those found in archaeological digs, so they presumably had a symbolic value as well.

The spear itself was also complex. It consisted of one long shaft with a shorter shaft attached at the front that also held the point. These foreshafts could be "reloaded," and apparently the hunter carried a number of them. They could also be fitted with different types and sizes of points, depending on the game being hunted.

Above: Atlatls in Coso rock art.

Left: Prehistoric atlatls recovered from a dry cave in Nevada.

Bottom: Foreshafts and points in hunter's bag, recovered from the same cave.

The hook to receive the spear is at top. The weight is shown much larger than in actual atlatls, which is clear when compared to the recovered atlatls shown on the previous page. The finger grip is the loop at the bottom.

Atlatls shown with conspicuously outsized throwing weights.

Female figure holding three atlatl foreshafts in her right hand. Incidentally, this is one of the few images that is clearly identifiable as a woman.

## BIGHORN SHEEP

**THE ATLATL WOULD HAVE** been used to hunt a large animal, and in the Coso range that animal would have been the bighorn sheep. Alan Gold thinks that the bighorn might have been as central to the Coso as the buffalo were to the Plains tribes or the salmon to the Northwest cultures.

It is said that there are approximately 20,000 images of bighorn, but it is impossible to find all of the petroglyphs. Many are tucked into the nooks and crannies of the canyons, and no one has attempted an exhaustive search.

Gold theorizes that the Coso must have had a sheep deity. Maybe they even believed that they were descended from the sheep and thought of themselves as "the people of the sheep."

I showed pictures of the sheep petroglyphs to a couple of big-game bow hunters. From practical experience, they know how difficult it is to approach and kill a bighorn. They suggested that maybe the petroglyphs were akin to the photos they would take of themselves after they had bagged a trophy animal. Knowing the challenge of hunting such an elusive animal, they suggested that maybe pecking the bighorn images on the rock was a young Coso man's announcement of coming of age after a successful hunt. In passing, they also mentioned that a bighorn makes a tasty meal.

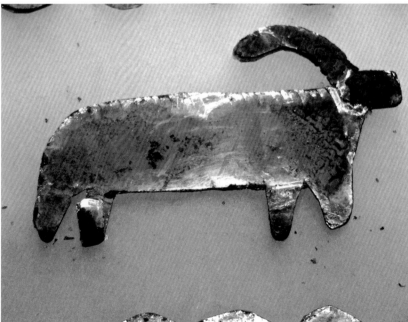

Ancient image of bighorn carved out of mica, from Arizona. Courtesy of Gilmer L. Brush.

Perhaps their interpretation of the images is accurate. Right or wrong, it is natural that the modern hunters would interpret these images in a way that made sense to them, using the context of their world. In fact, everyone I talked to seemed to interpret the images according to their personal life experience. Something about these images seems to make us want to "read" them. People seem to see them as a message of some sort and feel obligated (or hardwired) to connect to them.

Left: Atlatl images incised with giant weights and a bighorn image.

Hunters examine rock-art photos. They also theorized that there might have been an annual fall hunt, when the male bighorn came down from the mountains to rut and mate. They knew that at that time, bighorns would be the most vulnerable to a hunter, since they had only one thing in mind—sex. The hunters said that's when they themselves would have ambushed the sheep in canyons much like the ones covered with the petroglyphs.

Right: Bighorn hoof prints carved into the rock by the Coso.

# A WOMAN'S SITE

**SO FAR, ALL THE** rock art we had seen appeared to be associated with hunting or other mostly male activities. We asked to visit an area that might be more connected to women. Archaeologist Mike Baskerville took us onto the southern portion of the base. There we saw a noticeably different style of rock art. The landscape was different and the rock art looked different, even though it was only 50 miles from the Coso canyons. Baskerville said that it had been inhabited more recently—only in the last couple of thousand years—and probably by a culture more related to the Mojave tribes to the south and east. One feature was the rock formation at top right. From the side, it seems to resemble a rattlesnake head. Apparently, the ancient peoples also saw the similarity. In the "mouth," we found bedrock mortars that Mike said were probably for ritual use. It wasn't hard to imagine how impressive it would have looked with sage smoke seeping from the jaws while a shaman performed a ceremony.

Ritual bedrock mortars inside the "snake's mouth."

Mike Baskerville led us to an area by a small stream that had a number of deep, bedrock mortars. These, he said, were used for food processing by the women, and this was a woman's site. Nearby, on the vertical sides of the canyon walls were many very small indentations or cupules. Cupules like these appear in rock art all across the world and are believed to date back as far as the oldest forms. Alan Gold said there were ethnographic stories regarding historic use of these patterns. He had heard that they were the remnants of a ceremony, and the rock powder hammered out and removed from the cupules was then rubbed on a woman to promote fertility. In the rugged life of hunter-gatherers, the fertility rate was relatively low. In addition, a woman couldn't afford to have a new baby until her older child was able to walk on its own, since she could only carry one at a time when the group traveled between campsites. Maintaining families and population was a genuine challenge.

When we returned to the Coso canyons we could see evidence of cupules there as well, though not in such abundance.

Cupules pounded out of the sandstone.

Left: Bedrock mortars by creek.

# NEWBERRY CAVE

The museum storeroom.

**ALTHOUGH THE COSO DIDN'T** leave much of an archaeological record in the rock-art canyons, there was a trove of artifacts excavated in the 1950s from a dry cave not far away. The collection is now in storage in the San Bernardino County Museum in Redlands, California. This was our chance to see perishable items that could possibly have been part of the Coso world. While the cave is just outside what appears to have been Coso territory towards the Mojave Desert, we hoped that viewing the museum collection might help bring the Coso back to life—at least a little bit.

Newberry Cave is considered the largest cache ever found for this time period, dating to about 3,500 years ago (around the time of King Tutankhamun in Egypt). Gold arranged with curator Adella Schroth for us to go through the boxes of material stored in the museum. In her view, the cave was a repository for hunting material, a place to make repairs, and a site for ritual preparation before a hunt. It didn't seem to be lived in, only visited. Among the fragile items were a number of atlatl foreshafts, some broken, kept in the cave to be available for use in repairs, in addition to a quantity of stone and obsidian points. Beyond the functional items were some artifacts of less specific use. A number of partial and a few complete bighorn sheep effigies made from reeds were in the cave. A similarly made effigy, found in Nevada, had an arrowhead pushed into the body of the figure. Schroth said that it was thought that these effigies were probably used for hunting magic.

A unique find in Newberry Cave was a tiny, dried ball of organic material. On close examination, one can see it is cross-wrapped with very fine sinew. Analysis has shown it is a bighorn dropping. Perhaps a hunter wore it around his neck or carried it in a pouch, either during a ceremony or while on the hunt, reinforcing again the special status of the bighorn.

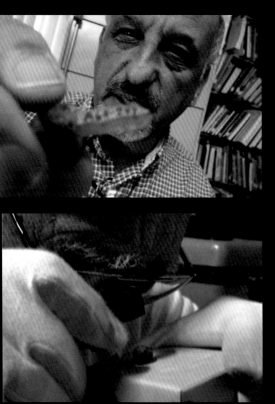

Don Austin and Alan Gold examine arrowheads found in Newberry Cave.

Tiny bighorn pellet (about a half-inch long) with sinew wrapping visible.

Newberry Cave Artifacts

Split-twig figures of bighorn sheep or deer

Three bighorn effigies from Newberry Cave.

Pieces of cane, which are either broken atlatl shafts or repair parts.

Portion of a sandal, made from tule, or large bulrush.

A wooden strip used as a fire starter. A stick would have been rapidly rotated in one of the burnt holes along with a little bit of tinder, dry moss, or reed, until it caught fire. Then it would have been spilled out to a larger collection of tinder gathered next to it. With great effort and lots of lungpower, a flame can be achieved.

# ABSTRACT IMAGES

Artist Tony Berlant in his studio.

**MANY OF THE OLDEST** images appear (at least to the modern eye) to be abstract. For some people, it is easy to speculate that this one is a snake or that one is a shield, but this would only be trying to make the images conform to our own concepts. No doubt, each image had a very specific meaning for its creator. We just don't know what that was—and probably never will.

Tony Berlant, the well-known Los Angeles artist who has spent years involved with and inspired by Native American art, thinks that abstract images emerged from visions. He posits that they came directly from the unconscious as a result of fasts, extended dance ceremonies, or a hallucinogenic agent. Historically, both tobacco and Jimsonweed (*Datura*) have been used to induce visions in religious ceremonies in California. Berlant points out that these abstract types of images are seen from the earliest cave paintings in Spain and France all the way through modern abstract painters. He calls these types of images "the alphabet of abstract art." From this perspective, the images (also known as entoptic phenomena or phosphenes) can be considered as embedded in our neurological system. Rather than pictures that are observed in the outside world, these images live inside our brains. Perhaps that is why they seem to be beckoning to us while remaining fundamentally foreign. We seem to know them, just not at a conscious level.

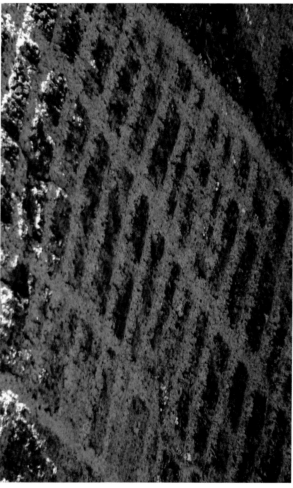

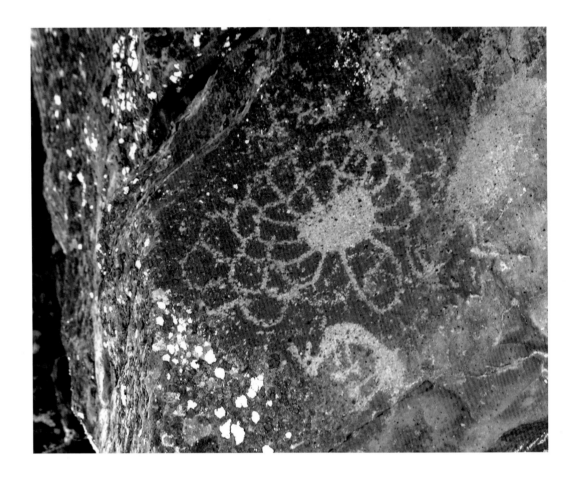

# PATTERNED-BODY ANTHROPOMORPHS

ANOTHER MAIN GROUP OF petroglyphs is standing figures. Anthropologists sometimes call them "patterned body anthropomorphs," or PBAs, in their lingo. When I heard this name, it struck me that anthropologists seem to go out of their way to use uninviting terminology. Whereas real estate agents give every new development, no matter how mundane its location, a romantic name like "Vista Del Mar" or "Apple Meadow Farm," anthropologists persist in sucking out the mystery. PBAs may be a dull name, but whatever you call them they are still intriguing characters.

The generally accepted theory is that the figures may be shamans or shamanic visions.

Left: What looks like a little purse dangling from the left hand of the figure in the foreground is thought to be a medicine man's or shaman's bundle—a collection of secret and sacred ritual objects. There are similar traditions in historic Southwestern cultures.

The figure appears to be holding an object in its right hand, perhaps a wand, mace, or prayer stick.

The south wall of Renegade Canyon. The images below are just visible at the bottom center of the canyon wall.

These figures certainly look scary, at least to my Western eye. Beth Kalish Weiss, a clinical psychologist, speculates that such images could be a way of externalizing the Cosos' fears. From a psychological perspective, if you take something that provokes fear and terror in you and bring it outside in some way (as in discussing it with a therapist), you can partially tame it. Putting it on a rock for all to see is certainly a way of transferring it to the external physical world. Dr. Weiss goes on to point out that for many indigenous cultures there is a melding of magical thinking into their reality. The world of hunter-gatherers was filled with predictable as well as unforeseen dangers, and perhaps these rock art images were a way of controlling such fears.

Beth Kalish Weiss.

Archaeologist Mike Baskerville has nicknamed this site "Monster Canyon" because of these intimidating figures.

Anthropologists think the patterns on these figures represent body painting or woven garments such as a blanket. The fabric theory is bolstered what appear to be fringes or tassels on the central image in the image on the opposite page.

# SIDE TRIP TO A MORE RECENT SITE

**ALAN GOLD THINKS SOME** of these patterned-body anthropomorphs may be depictions of the Animal Master. He explained to me that a shared concept in many Native American cultures is the idea that game animals never die; they just go away and exist underground or elsewhere until the Animal Master recalls them each spring.

To explain the idea of the Animal Master, he took me to a cave not far from the Coso area that is considered by the Kawaiisu to be where the animals reemerge or are reborn. Here the images are painted (not pecked) and are much more recent, so recent that there is some direct knowledge about their meaning. Alan heard some of these stories from a Kawaiisu elder, Harold Williams, and we visited the cave because he thought the Coso might have had similar beliefs. Alan showed me rock-painting images that he said were placed there to protect the spiritual site. These he could interpret since the Kawaiisu and Harold Williams were still around to answer questions. The central story seemed to be one of the annual rebirth of animals. The bear and snake images were there to protect the cave. Alan said the cave had been the site of ceremonies and a power site for a sha-man. Could the Coso canyons have some similarities?

Harold Williams.

Back in the Coso canyons, we looked at the image above and wondered if it represented a shaman wearing a bighorn headdress. It is certainly some sort of conflation of human body and a horned head. A couple of bighorn headdresses have survived in dry caves, as seen on the opposite page. Originally the headdresses would have had a full cap with earflaps and sinew to tie it firmly to the wearer's head. Over the years, rodents have eaten almost the entire hide, leaving just the top horn portion.

Bighorn sheep shrine found at Rose Spring site, California (Coso area). Drawing by Michael W. Chittock.

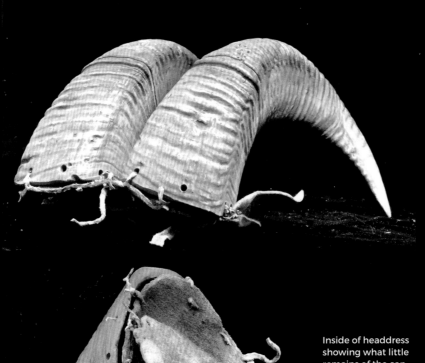

Inside of headdress showing what little remains of the cap and ties.

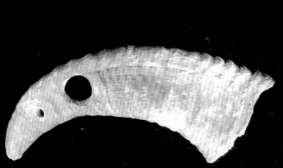

Arrow shaft straightener made from bighorn.

Frames from the 1914 film *Land of the Headhunters* made by Edward Curtis. Shot in British Columbia, where some Native American ceremonies had survived long enough to be filmed, this may give a glimpse of the sort of rituals that were enacted in the Coso canyons.

# A NATIVE AMERICAN'S PERSPECTIVE

Ron Wermuth.

**TOWARD THE END OF** our filming, I talked to Ron Wermuth, a Kern Native, who still came onto the Coso land for traditional religious purposes. He projected a strong, confident connection to the Coso landscape. When I spoke to him, we were wreathed in steam from the Coso hot springs where Ron had come for a ritual. The site was sacred to him, and I have not included any photos of the hot springs in this book. When I asked what he understood to be the meaning of the petroglyphs, I expected some sort of inside vision of Native American knowledge or perhaps a refusal to say anything at all. Instead, Ron was quick to say that he didn't know what they meant; all that mattered to him was that they were there and he felt a connection to them. End of conversation.

Ron died a few months later, and I dedicated the film to him.

The swept-back ears and long tail suggest a mountain lion.

Lizards or horned toads.

# DATING THE PETROGLYPHS

Humboldt point made from obsidian.

**SINCE PETROGLYPHS ARE MADE** by removing stone, there is nothing organic to date. There have been attempts made to determine the age of the repatination that forms on the pecked areas, but so far it is just guesswork. In some cases, the objects portrayed allow an estimate of the age. The Christmas tree-like shapes in the figures on the opposite page are representations of a certain type of atlatl spear point called "Humboldt."

This particular type of point dates from the period 3,500 years ago to about 1,500 years ago, so it can be assumed the image was made during that time span. While this is not very exact, it can help date images that are older or younger.

Although only the roughest dates can be guessed, it is clear which images were pecked first and which overlays. The underlying images are thousands of years older and often are very faint. By using a computer application called DStretch, developed by Jon Harman, new versions can be produced with bright artificial colors that enhance and reveal the earlier images. The large, colorful photo on the opposite page is a DStretch version of the smaller, unreduced one shown above.

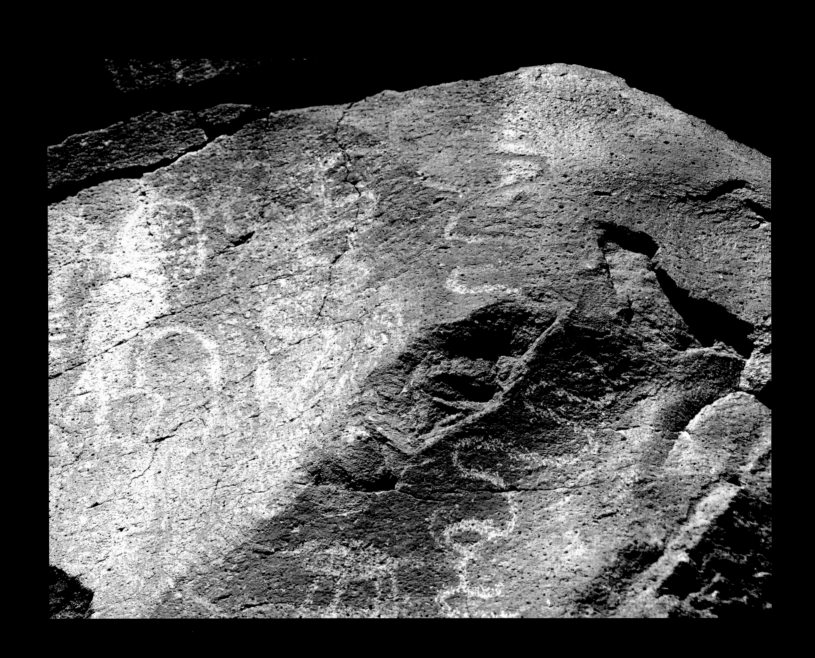

In studying these petroglyphs, I've often noticed that much more material is pecked out than required for the simple outline. For the petroglyph at upper right, a lot of effort went into removing the interior of the image. Could it be that the process of pecking the rock art was as sacred as the final product? It brings to mind the effort and decades-long dedication involved in building medieval European cathedrals.

Believed to be the image of a hunting dog.

# THE ANTHROPOLOGISTS' HYPOTHESIS

**WHY ARE SO MANY** petroglyphs concentrated in such a small area? For what purpose? Alan Gold's hypothesis (and he's not alone here) is that there was a sort of perfect storm. As hunter-gatherers, the Coso had always depended on a yearly cycle of rebirth, new plants, seeds, roots, and animals. This in turn was affected by the weather and the amount the Coso hunted and gathered in each year. There had to be a balance, and Alan thinks that when the bow and arrow were introduced some 1,500 years ago, the Coso became much more proficient hunters. The image to the right also suggests that they may have added the dog to their hunting, a partner that could substantially increase their chances of success. The plants and animals may also have been under additional pressure from new peoples moving into the area, and a stretch of drought may also have exacerbated the entire situation. As the bighorn became more rare, it would have become an even more prestigious trophy, causing it to be hunted with increasing intensity.

According to this hypothesis, the many sheep petroglyphs are a sort of visual prayer, a desire or a plea to bring back the bighorn—perhaps addressed to the Animal Master, perhaps to the sheep, or some other power. It's just a hypothesis, but we do know that the Coso disappeared from these canyons and mountains along with the bighorn.

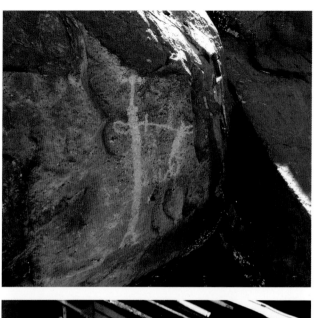

Desert bows from the Navy collection.

The curled arm represents the hunter drawing the bowstring. When the bow and arrow appear in the rock art, the atlatl disappears. It would be scientifically pleasing to find a bow hunter pecked on top of an atlatl petroglyph, but I don't know of one.

The bow hunter had several advantages over the spear thrower. He could crouch and remain hidden, and he could reload and fire rapidly. The improved efficiency of this technology resulted in the complete replacement of the atlatl.

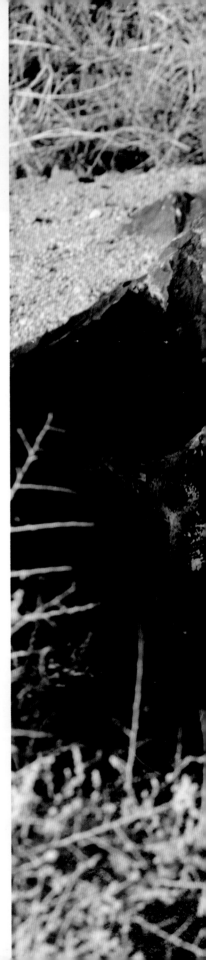

Possibly the bottom of a bighorn's hoofs with the rest of the image in profile.

Another example of pecking across the entire pattern.

# THE RETURN OF THE BIGHORN

**AS WE WERE FINISHING** our filming in the summer of 2013, Alan Gold and I met with Base Commanding Officer, Captain Dennis Lazar. A surprise to us, we found out he was an enthusiastic supporter of the Navy's protecting and curating the unique cultural resources that happened to be on his weapons-testing site. He had visited the canyons a number of times and even had trained to become a docent to lead tours. One canyon is open to small groups organized by Alan and also by the Maturango Museum located in Ridgecrest, California. Independent groups can get permission from the naval base. In the spring and fall, a couple of dozen visits are permitted but just to one canyon. I was impressed that the Navy valued and supported these cultural resources right up to and including the Commanding Officer, who functions very much as the CEO of the military base.

We talked with Captain Lazar about the meanings of the rock art. Alan offered his ideas and then said that Ron Wermuth, the Kern Native we met earlier, would like to try to bring the bighorn back. Ron had been praying for their return. Captain Lazar became excited. Clearly he saw that as a challenge but something the Navy could help accomplish. In language befitting a military man, he said that if this could be done, "It would be a huge victory." But at that moment he began what will no doubt be a long, careful process requiring cooperation from a number of parties. Still, it is just possible that the message that these ancient images have held for so many years will be heard today, and the bighorn will return to the Coso Mountains.

Captain Dennis Lazar, Commanding Officer, Naval Air Weapons Station China Lake.

# AUTHOR'S NOTE

**AFTER SPENDING A COUPLE** of years on the film and book project, I succumbed like everyone else to dreaming up my own hypothesis. I don't have any perceptions on the images themselves. What interests me is how interested everyone else is in the rock art. Arrowheads, baskets, and metates rarely intrigue my friends, but when I show them pictures of rock art just about everyone is engaged. They peer at the images intently and seem to feel impelled to react or interpret them. I wonder why.

During the time it took me to make the film and book, I was also involved in a project about "consciousness" and neuroscience. Listening to scientists discuss what they know and don't know about the brain taught me just how much our behavior is determined by our brain structure. I got to thinking about the ancient rock art and contemporary responses. Could it be that a part of our brain had been sensitized to "reading" images long before we had alphabets or hieroglyphs? Perhaps over tens of thousands of years of looking at hoof prints, animal tracks, forest trails, clouds, water surfaces, and who-knows-what, humans built up an area in the brain that was primed for and instantly engaged with these signs. Perhaps when writing came along it built on that part of the brain. And perhaps when we look at rock art today that older part of our brain can't resist firing and becoming engaged. It is awakened, and we produce our varied interpretations to try to satisfy the ancient urge. Just an idea.

# SUGGESTIONS

**THE BOOK YOU HAVE** just read was designed to be primarily a visual experience.

In preparing the pages, I learned that even the least amount of text (such as location name or date) can divert the eye from the image and somehow the experience changes. To this end, I have provided as little explanation or analysis as possible.

If these images have piqued your interest and you would like to know more about Coso rock art, here are some of the titles I have consulted and the anthropologists who have spent all or a large part of their careers teasing out information. There is also a set of references at the end of this book.

*Alan Gold*, the archaeologist seen in this book, leads tours into China Lake along with providing a day of classes in his program Rock Art 101. Find information on this class through the California Rock Art Foundation (http://www. carockart.org). Alan has spent his entire professional life studying Coso petroglyphs.

The only canyon open for the occasional guided tour is Little Petroglyph Canyon. Trips are in spring and fall. Alan's trips are usually on a Sunday after a Saturday presentation, lecture, and film that he arranges in a hotel in Ridgecrest. Some of the images in this book come from Little Petroglyph Canyon. A day spent—more likely half a day because of the long drive to the canyon and back—walking the canyon will definitely give you the experience

of personally encountering these petroglyphs.

I have found that the experience is both more magical than you might expect yet somehow familiar. The experience is magical because you are in the remote high desert with no trace of modern man, exploring the boulders and canyon at your own pace, discovering the images for yourself, everywhere. The experience is familiar because the rock art is concentrated in this one place and is clearly meant to be viewed. The presentation has a very human scale, sort of a Times Square of images, but instead of blinking signs and giant billboards, it is carefully pecked stone. Although what they are saying is not very accessible, the instinct to make these images seems familiar. One can imagine a brotherhood with the image-makers.

Alan Gold has founded the California Rock Art Foundation (http://www.carockart.org), whose website gives more information regarding trips to China Lake and preservation activities. Also see his book *Archaeology and Rock Art of the Eastern Sierra and Great Basin Frontier*.

*The Maturango Museum in Ridgecrest* is the local museum (China Lake is adjacent to Ridgecrest) and it provides tours with docents Maturango Museum, 100 East Las Flores Avenue, Ridgecrest, CA 93555; (760) 375–6900, http://www.maturango.org.

*David Whitley* is a name that usually comes up when Coso petroglyphs are discussed. His book *Introduction to Rock Art Research* was first published in 2005 and offers a good introduction to the study of rock art. He also published an earlier book, *The Art of the Shaman*, that contains Coso imagery. Of his books, my favorite is *Cave Paintings and the Human Spirit: The Origin of Creativity and Belief*. While it is not specifically on rock art, it captures the mystery that attracts us to ancient imagery.

*Jo Anne Van Tilburg*, a UCLA professor, has coedited an exhaustive study of Coso rock art at Little Lake, which is adjacent to the Navy property and is the only privately owned land that has imagery in common. Her book is *Rock Art at Little Lake: An Ancient Crossroads in the California Desert*. She also has authored a book on California rock art, *Ancient Images On Stone: Rock Art of the Californias*, the first published book on the Coso canyons (1983).

*Campbell Grant, James Baird*, and *J. Kenneth Pringle* offer *Rock Drawings of the Coso Range, Inyo County, California: An Ancient Sheep-Hunting Cult Pictured in Desert Rock Carvings* through the Maturango Museum.

*Coso Rock Art: A New Perspective*, edited by *Elva Younkin*, describes changes and advances in dating and interpreting rock art and focuses on the Cosos. Chapters are by David Whitley and other experts in the field. It contains many photos and illustrations, including several color plates. Lastly, there is *Talking Stone: Rock Art of the Cosos*, a Paul Goldsmith Film, 53 minutes, (2014). The documentary covers the same material as this book in an informal style that is the next best thing to an actual visit to the Coso canyons. It is available as a DVD or can be downloaded through the Bradshaw Foundation, which specializes in international rock art (http://www.bradshawfoundation.com); Documentary Educational Resources (DER), Watertown, Massachusetts, is a major distributor of anthropological films: alijah@der.org.

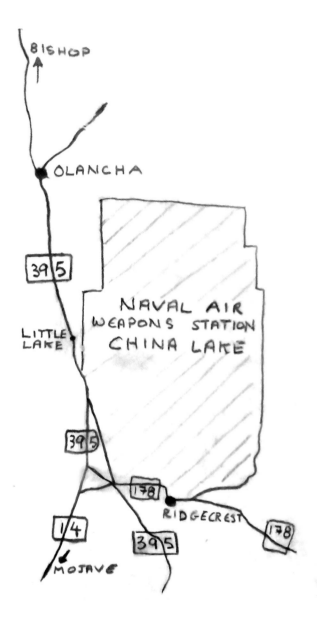

# REFERENCES

Gold, Alan Garfinkel

2007   *Archaeology and Rock Art of the Eastern Sierra and Great Basin Frontier.* Maturango Press. Ridgecrest, CA.

Goldsmith, Paul

2014   *Talking Stone: Rock Art of the Cosos.* A Paul Goldsmith Film, Distributed by the Bradshaw Foundation, Geneva, Switzerland (http://www.bradshawfoundation.com), and Documentary Educational Resources (DER), Watertown, MA (alijah@der.org). DVD and download, 53 minutes.

Grant, Campbell, James W. Baird, and J. Kenneth Pringle

1987   *Rock Drawings of the Coso Range, Inyo County, California: An Ancient Sheep-Hunting Cult Pictured in Desert Rock Carvings.* Publication No. 4. Maturango Press, Ridgecrest, CA.

Van Tilburg, Jo Anne (editor)

1983   *Ancient Images On Stone: Rock Art of the Californias.* Cotsen Institute of Archaeology Press. Los Angeles, CA.

Van Tilburg, Jo Anne, John Bretney, and Gordon Hull (editors)

2012   *Rock Art at Little Lake: An Ancient Crossroads in the California Desert.* Cotsen Institute of Archaeology Press. Los Angeles, CA.

Whitley, David S.

2000   *The Art of the Shaman.* University of Utah Press. Salt Lake City, UT.

2011 [2005] *Introduction to Rock Art Research*, 2nd ed. Left Coast Press. Davis, CA.

Younkin, Elva (editor)

1998   *Coso Rock Art: A New Perspective.* Maturango Press. Ridgecrest, CA.

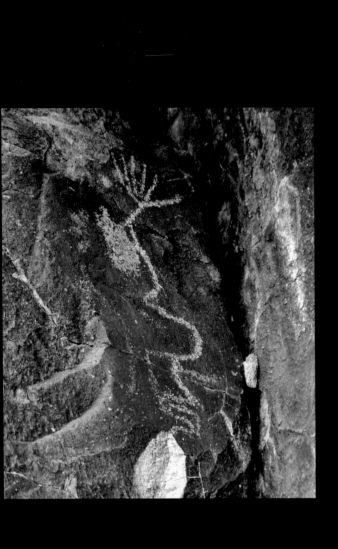

# THANKS

Alan P. Garfinkel Gold, PhD, anthropologist
Naval Air Weapons Station China Lake (NAWS)
Peggy Shoaf, A CIV NAWS PAO
Mike Baskerville, NAWSCL, archaeologist
Commanding Officer Capt. Dennis Lazar, NAWS
Commanding Officer Capt. Rich Wiley, NAWS
Beth Kalish Weiss, clinical psychologist
Tony Berlant, artist
Justin Farmer, Ipai Native
Harold Williams, Kawaiisu Elder
Ron Wermuth, Kern Native
Dick Agin, Dan Agin, Kody Dietrich, Alan Panoli, hunters
Sandy Rogers, curator, Maturango Museum
Charles White, director, Tehachapi Heritage League
Leonard Feinstein, editor
Allen Alsobrook
Dwayne Horii, Little Lake Duck Hunting Club
Adella Schroth, curator, San Bernardino County Museum
Timothy and Jean Schmit
Jack Pritchett
Michael Heumann
John Evans, Diesel Books
Peta Goldsmith, editor
Kristen Hilton, editor
Alice, Rebecca, and Columbine Goldsmith
Rebecca Rauch, acquisitions editor, University of Utah Press